LEARN HOW TO PLAY APPALACHIAN DULCIMER BEGINNERS GUIDE

A Step-By-Step Guide For Beginners To Mastering Learn, Play, And Perfect Your Skills With Easy-To-Follow Lessons, Chords, And Tunes

ROLANDO NEWMAN

pg. 1

Table of Contents

You are about to go on a musical voyage that will take you to Appalachia's rolling hills and foggy mountains. With its enchanting, melodic tones, the Appalachian dulcimer is more than just a musical instrument; it's a doorway to a rich cultural past and a vehicle for individual expression.

You may experience a mixture of anxiety and exhilaration when you first hold this exquisite instrument in your hands. But do not worry! Part of the dulcimer's appeal is its simplicity.

Despite being one of the simplest stringed instruments to learn, its diatonic fretboard and drone strings allow for endless melodic exploration.

Picture yourself lounging on a porch as the sun is setting and the warm tones of your dulcimer blend with the fading day's glory. You're conveying tales, stirring feelings, and establishing a connection with countless musicians who have found comfort and delight in these same tunes as your fingers dance over the strings—you're doing more than just playing an instrument.

The long history of the Appalachian dulcimer matches the richness of its musical output.

This instrument, which originated in the Appalachian Mountains, has accompanied many people faithfully throughout history, from pioneers to contemporary musicians. Its soft voice has cheered happy events, comforted hurting hearts, and safeguarded the oral traditions of a distinctly American culture.

Acquiring proficiency on the dulcimer goes beyond mere technique; it's about delving into a vast repertoire of hymns, folk songs, and modern works. You will discover that this seemingly straightforward instrument has depths you could never have imagined as you advance.

You'll learn new techniques for playing, try out various tunings, and maybe even write original music.

It makes me think of my Uncle Jim, who took up the dulcimer as a retirement hobby. Though he had never played an instrument before, he was playing the guitar at family get-togethers in a few months, his proud and happy expression shining.

Not only did the dulcimer provide him with a new interest, but it also made him feel unexpectedly closer to our family's Appalachian heritage.

Thus, keep in mind that every note you play is a step into a realm of music, history, and self-discovery as we embark on this adventure together. The Appalachian dulcimer is a tool that can help you connect with a thriving musical tradition and unleash your creativity.

CHAPTER 1

Greetings from the amazing world of dulcimers. It's likely that if you're reading this book, you're either inquisitive about this endearing instrument or have already become enamored with its lovely, melodic sounds. You're in for a treat either way! With a specific emphasis on the star of the show, the Appalachian dulcimer, let's explore the dulcimer's intriguing history, cultural significance, and distinctive qualities.

A Walk Down Memory Lane: The Dulcimer's History and Origins

Imagine if hundreds of years ago, somewhere in the old world, someone came up with the wonderful notion to cover a resonating box with strings. And voilà! Our beloved dulcimer's oldest ancestor was born. The dulcimer's "birthday" is unknown, although we may trace its ancestry to ancient stringed instruments from many different cultures.

The word "dulcimer" itself derives from the Latin words "dulce" (sweet) and "melos" (sound), which well describes the soft, calming tones of the instrument. However, dulcimers have roots throughout the world, so don't let the Latin fool you.

Early dulcimer variations in Europe were known as "psaltery" throughout the Middle Ages. These varied-sized and shaped instruments could be strummed or plucked. The hammered dulcimer originated when individuals began experimenting with striking the strings rather than plucking them over time.

German, Scottish, and Irish immigrants carried their musical traditions to America while they were over the pond. These customs combined with inventiveness from the area to form what is now known as the Appalachian dulcimer in the Appalachian region. Since its invention in the early 1800s, this unusual instrument—also known as the lap dulcimer or mountain dulcimer—has captured people's hearts.

Cultural Importance and Development: Beyond a Simple Musical Note

Let's now discuss why the dulcimer is so much more than simply a nice face (or sound) in the music industry. This tool has been crucial in maintaining and forming cultural identities in many geographical areas.

The dulcimer became an essential component of folk music traditions in the Appalachian Mountains. Its mellow, droning tone went well with the folk melodies and stories about love, grief, and mountain living. Frequently crafted by hand, the instrument was handed down through the generations and performed at social events, eventually turning into a representation of Appalachian culture and tenacity.

Similar cultural significance was attributed to dulcimer variants in different parts of the world. For example, the hammered dulcimer has long been a mainstay of Persian, Turkish, and Indian classical music. It is commonly used in folk and classical music and is referred to as the cimbalom in Eastern Europe.

The dulcimer changed over time in tandem with shifting musical preferences and advances in technology. The folk music renaissance of the mid-1900s revived interest in traditional instruments, such as the Appalachian dulcimer. Beyond just folk music, musicians started experimenting with other playing styles and utilizing the dulcimer in other genres.

Dulcimers may still be heard in a wide range of genres these days, from modern pop to traditional folk music, demonstrating their versatility.

A Family Get-Together: Various Dulcimers

Okay, so we've covered the history. Let me now introduce you to the various Dulcimer family tree branches. Although the Appalachian dulcimer will be the main subject of this book, it's good getting to know its cousins:

1. Imagine a trapezoid-shaped sound box with multiple strings stretched across it to represent a hammered dulcimer. To produce a loud, percussive sound, players strike the strings with small hammers or mallets. It's portable, just like a piano!

2. The Appalachian Dulcimer is the main attraction! Usually, this instrument has three or four strings that run the length of its long, narrow body. It is typically played with a pick and a note, which is a little stick, on a table or on one's lap.

3. Close cousins of the Appalachian dulcimer, the German Scheitholt, and the Nordic Langeleik have diatonic fretboards and long, narrow bodies.

They are still played in their respective locations and are thought to be the forefathers of the Appalachian dulcimer.

4. Cimbalom: A more ornate, bigger dulcimer that is well-liked in Hungary and the neighboring nations. It is frequently heard in Romani music and orchestral settings.

Though each of these instruments has its charm and manner of playing, they all have that endearing dulcimer sound in common.

The Appalachian Dulcimer: Why Select It? Count the ways with me!

"With all these wonderful options, why should I choose the Appalachian dulcimer?" you ask.

Well, my friend, this little instrument has a lot of power! The Appalachian dulcimer could end up being your new best buddy for the following reasons:

Special characteristics and sound: The Appalachian dulcimer has a distinct tone. Its drone strings provide the music with a steady, calming background that gives it a unique, almost mesmerizing character. Even for novices, the instrument's diatonic fretboard facilitates straightforward tuning. And let's not overlook its aesthetic appeal: the Appalachian dulcimer is as much a work of art as it is a musical instrument, thanks to its long, thin body and exquisite craftsmanship.

Beginners' Friendly Simplicity and Accessibility: If you've ever picked up an instrument and exclaimed, "Wow, this is complicated!", do not be alarmed! The Appalachian dulcimer is very approachable for novices.

It's easy to start composing music right away thanks to its straightforward interface and design. You don't have to be a skilled finger dexter or learn intricate chord structures. You can quickly become proficient at strumming songs with a few simple approaches.

For many people, the dulcimer's lap-playing position is an additional benefit. It's easy to handle and doesn't necessitate the occasionally uncomfortable positions needed for other instruments. Because of this, individuals of all ages and physical capabilities can use it.

Versatility across Musical Genres: The Appalachian dulcimer is a musical chameleon, despite its traditional roots.

Although it excels in folk and traditional music, inventive players have used it to play a wide range of genres, including rock, classical, and even experimental.

It can be used as a solo instrument or as an accompaniment to singing because of its delicate, pleasant tone. The dulcimer is a versatile instrument that can play hymns, modern melodies, Celtic music, and old-time Appalachian tunes.

A Personal Touch: Playing an instrument with such a deep cultural and historical background is truly unique. Taking up an Appalachian dulcimer allows you to engage with a legacy that crosses generations and continents in addition to creating music. It's a means to both preserve and personalize cultural heritage.

In addition, the dulcimer community is among the friendliest, most inviting communities you will ever come across. Dulcimists are always willing to share their knowledge, advice, and songs with novices, whether it's at festivals or on internet forums.

That is our brief overview of the cultural significance, history, and reasons to fall in love with the Appalachian dulcimer. We'll get further into the specifics of playing this endearing instrument as we go through this book.

The Appalachian dulcimer has something special to offer, regardless of your level of experience as a musician and your desire to expand your repertoire.

CHAPTER 2

Now that you've made the decision to take up the dulcimer as your new instrument, it's time to get to know it better. If it seems a little daunting at first, don't worry; by the conclusion of this chapter, you'll know every part of your dulcimer by name. Now let's get started and investigate this amazing instrument together!

The Dulcimer's Anatomy

You know how it's said that to be a master of your trade, one must know their tools? That also applies to musical instruments. Let's disassemble the dulcimer to discover what goes into making this lovely instrument work.

The dulcimer's components and their purposes

1. The soundboard, which is often composed of cedar or spruce, is the face of your dulcimer. It's

the big, level area that appears when you see the instrument from above.

Because it intensifies the sound of the strings, the soundboard is essential. See it as the megaphone of the dulcimer!

2. Strings: Three or four strings are found on most dulcimers. These are the main performers; you'll be plucking, strumming, or pounding them to produce those lovely songs. Usually, steel or a combination of steel and brass is used to make the strings.

3. The raised section close to the bottom of the soundboard, known as the bridge, is what holds up the strings and allows their vibrations to be transferred to the board. Your dulcimer would sound about as melodic without the bridge as a rubber band draped over a shoebox!

4. Nut: The nut is located at the other end of the bridge. It's a little strip that supports the strings at the instrument's head and is sometimes composed of hard plastic or bone.

The nut aids in determining the strings' playable length.

5. The knobs at the top of the instrument are called tuning pegs, and you'll use them to tune your dulcimer. Their mechanism of action is altering the string tension.

6. The lengthy section of the instrument's midsection marked with metal frets is called the fretboard. We'll cover this topic in greater detail later!

7. The ornamental holes on the soundboard are called sound holes. They contribute to sound projection and give your dulcimer a unique voice.

8. The instrument's body is made up of the sides and back. Usually constructed from hardwoods like mahogany, walnut, or cherry, they aid in dulcimer tone shaping.

Recognizing the fretboard

Now that we have focused on the fretboard, let's see what magic is all about! The metal strips known as frets divide the fretboard into different parts. Every fret denotes a distinct note, and the notes increase higher in pitch as you proceed up the fretboard (in the direction of the bridge).

One neat feature of the dulcimer is that you only need to touch the string to the fret, as opposed to pressing the string down to the fretboard on a guitar.

This facilitates playing, particularly for those who are inexperienced or have arthritis.

Due to their diatonic fretboards, most dulcimers are only designed to play in one key. If that seems restrictive, don't worry—you'd be surprised at how many songs you can play in only one key!

many sizes and forms

Dulcimers are made in many shapes and sizes, much like individuals. Hourglass-shaped dulcimers are the most popular, but you can also find teardrop- or even rectangular-shaped ones.

A normal dulcimer's length is typically between 30 and 34 inches, but larger and smaller models are also available—perfect for traveling musicians or children, for example.

The sound of a dulcimer can vary depending on its size; larger dulcimers typically have a richer, deeper tone, while smaller dulcimers tend to be brighter.

Selecting Your Initial Dulcimer

Now that you understand the components of a dulcimer, let's discuss how to select your own. Although this step is exhilarating, it can also be a little intimidating. But don't worry, I've got you covered!

Things to think about before purchasing a dulcimer

1. Sound is the most crucial component. Each dulcimer has a distinct voice of its own.

While some are warm and soothing, others are clear and bright. Choose a dulcimer that makes your heart sing after listening to a few different ones.

2. Playability: Verify that holding and playing the dulcimer is comfortable.

If the action (the space between the strings and the fretboard) is too high, it will be difficult to apply pressure to the strings.

3. Build quality: Seek for a well-constructed device. Playing should not produce any buzzing, the joints should be tight, and the finish should be smooth.

4. Wood: The kind of wood you use can have an impact on your dulcimer's appearance and tone. Spruce, cedar, cherry, and walnut are common woods. Everyone has distinct tonal qualities.

5. The majority of dulcimers are equipped with three or four strings. Four-string dulcimers are more versatile than three-string dulcimers, which are traditional and excellent for folk music.

6. Cost: The price range of dulcimers varies, with basic models costing less than $100 and high-end instruments exceeding $1000.

You certainly don't need to spend a lot of money on a top-of-the-line model if you're just starting, but it's still worthwhile to get a good instrument that will develop with you as you gain experience.

Buying vs. renting

Are you unsure if you're ready to make the purchase of a dulcimer? Renting could be a wise choice.

You can rent an instrument from several music stores and test it out for a few months. This might be a really cost-effective method of determining whether the dulcimer is the perfect instrument for you.

Make sure to enquire about rent-to-own alternatives if you do want to rent. In the event that you decide to buy the instrument later, certain retailers may credit your rental payments toward the purchase price.

Crucial add-ons: stands, picks, and cases

After obtaining your dulcimer, you should consider purchasing the following extras:

1. Picks: To play your dulcimer, you'll need these. Start by experimenting with a variety pack to see what fits the best. Flat picks can also be used; however, many dulcimer players prefer to use thumb and finger picks.

2. Case: To keep your instrument safe, a quality case is a must. Hard cases provide greater protection, but soft cases are less expensive and lighter.

3. Stand: You can securely put your dulcimer down in between performances with the help of a stand. It's also a fantastic way to show off your gorgeous new dulcimer!

4. Tuner: To keep your dulcimer in tune, use an electronic tuner. Some even fit your instrument like a glove.

5. Extra strings: Having an extra set of strings on hand is a good idea because they can break.

6. Strap: A strap is essential if you intend to play while standing.

Folks, there you have it! Now that you know everything there is to know about dulcimers, you may make your own selections. Never forget that enjoying yourself with your new instrument is what matters most.

The dulcimer that inspires you to compose music is ultimately the greatest, so don't get too wrapped up on the details.

CHAPTER 3

We've arrived at one of the most important sections of your dulcimer learning process. Yes, we are delving into the realm of tuning. You may be thinking, "Tuning? Isn't that just twisting some pegs until it sounds right?" But, my friend, there's a little more to it than that, and you'll become an expert at it by the end of this chapter!

Knowledge of Dulcimer Tuning

Let's begin with the fundamentals. Your dulcimer gains a voice when it is tuned. We need to tune our dulcimers so they're prepared to sing their lovely melodies, just like vocalists warm up their vocal cords. But first, let's discuss the significance of tuning before getting into the specifics.

You see, a dulcimer that is in tune not only sounds better, but it is also more manageable to play.

The rich, rich sound that dulcimers are known for is produced when the strings vibrate in unison with one another when they are in tune. Playing in tune also trains your ear, which improves your overall musicianship. I promise that your audience and bandmates will appreciate you taking the time to warm up!

Principles of Tuning a Dulcimer

Okay, let's get to the point. Usually, a mountain dulcimer has three or four strings, and each string has to be tuned to a certain note. "DAD" tuning is the most widely used tuning.

No, it's not called after your dad, even though he might find it amusing. When you tune a string DAD (the string nearest to you when playing) signifies that the middle string is tuned to A, the far string back to D, and the first string to D.

The intriguing part is that there are a lot of tuning options available for the dulcimer. Dulcimers can be tuned in a variety of ways to accommodate different songs or playing styles, in contrast to some other instruments that have a "standard" tuning. One of the qualities that makes the dulcimer so special and enjoyable to play is this!

Typical Tunings

Let's examine a few of the most widely used tuning choices:

1. As previously noted, DAD tuning (D-A-D) is the most popular tune. It's perfect for novices as it's simple to pick up and fits nicely with a variety of songs, particularly in the key of D.

2. DAA Tuning (D-A-A): This tuning is commonly used when performing in the D or G key. Compared to DAD, it produces a brighter tone, and Celtic and traditional music frequently use it.

3. The DGD tuning, or D-G-D, is excellent for playing in the key of G. Folk and bluegrass music frequently use it.

4. The AEA tuning (A-E-A) is your best friend while performing music in the key of A. Celtic and Appalachian music frequently employ it.

5. CGC Tuning (C-G-C): Your dulcimer will sound richer and deeper with this lower tuning, which is excellent for tunes in the key of C.

Recall that these are but a few instances. Try out a few different tunings as you become more familiar with your instrument. Who knows? You could even come up with your own!

How to Tune by Ear and Use a Tuner

Let's now discuss how to tune your dulcimer properly. There are two primary approaches: tuning by ear or with an electronic tuner.

How to Use an Electronic Tuner

The simplest approach is this one, especially for newcomers. Most music stores and online retailers carry reasonably priced clip-on tuners. How to utilize one is as follows:

1. Attach the tuner to the headstock of your dulcimer.

2. Grab a string and pluck it.

3. You can see which note the string is playing on the tuner, as well as if it's flat (too low) or sharp (too high).

4. Once the tuner indicates that you are on the correct note, adjust the tuning peg.

5. For every string, repeat.

Never forget to tune your other strings about your central string, which is often A.

Aural tuning:

Although it requires more effort, learning this technique is a useful ability. This is a fundamental method:

1. To get your middle A string in tune, use a reference tone (such as a tuning fork, piano, or other instrument).

2. Play the seventh fret on the A string after your A string is in tune. This ought to be in tune with your high D string.

As necessary, make adjustments.

3. Play your low D string at the seventh fret. The open A string should correspond to this. To make the low D match, adjust.

You'll learn to detect when strings are in tune with one another as you practice. It's similar to becoming a superhero in music!

Sustaining Your Harmony

Now that you have your dulcimer tuned, all right. Well done, I hope. Not exactly, though. Maintaining the tuning of your dulcimer is a continuous task. The following advice can assist you in keeping that flawless pitch:

Frequent Tuning Procedures

1. Tune every time you play: Develop the practice of always checking your tuning before you begin. It may make a huge impact in just one minute.

2. Retune during longer sessions: Depending on the humidity and temperature variations, your strings may become slightly out of tune when you play for extended periods. Every thirty minutes or so, give them a short check.

3. Extra care is required for new strings.

If you have just changed your strings, you should anticipate returning more frequently in the initial days while the strings adjust and stretch.

4. Be gentle: Make only minor tweaks while fine-tuning. Your instrument or even your strings may get damaged if you overtighten them.

Handling Tuning Problems

Even with the best of intentions, tuning issues can occasionally arise. Fear not; it occurs to the best of us. The following are some typical problems and solutions:

1. When strings become out of tune, it could be because they are new and have not yet settled, or it could be a sign that there is an issue with your tuning pegs. Verify if they are sufficiently tight to support tension.

2. Make sure the string is correctly positioned in the nut and bridge since one string always goes flat. Tuning problems may arise from a string slipping occasionally.

3. Fret buzz: If you're playing and you hear a buzzing sound, there may not be a tuning problem at all. Verify if your strings are contacting the frets or are set too low. It may be necessary to modify your bridge.

4. Extreme variations in humidity or temperature might have an impact on the tuning of your dulcimer. Make an effort to keep your instrument in a steady place.

5. Uneven tuning across the fretboard: You may need to alter the bridge if your dulcimer sounds good when played on open strings but not so much when played up the neck. You may need to see a professional for "intonation" if you feel uneasy performing it on your own.

Recall that tuning is both a science and an art. You'll become more adept at discerning those minute variations and maintaining the finest possible sounding dulcimer with continued practice.

Folks, there you have it! With this newfound understanding, you can continue to play your dulcimer melodically. If it looks difficult at first, don't give up; tuning is a skill that requires practice. You'll be tuning up quicker than you can say "Appalachian string music" before you know it!

CHAPTER 4

Now that we've reached Chapter 4, let's get started with some fundamental music theory. If the word "theory" makes you a little uneasy, don't worry; we'll keep things lighthearted and easy. Let's get started! Mastering these foundational concepts will greatly aid in your development as a dulcimer musician.

An Overview of Musical Scales and Notes

Let's start by talking about musical notes. You've probably noticed the tiny black dots on sheet music. The fundamental units of all music are those notes. Every note denotes a distinct pitch or the volume of a sound.

The seven primary notes in Western music, which is what we're concentrating on here, are A, B, C, D, E, F, and G. When you adjust the pitch, these repeat in a cycle. Every fret on your dulcimer corresponds to a distinct note.

The notes increase higher in pitch as you move your finger up the fretboard, nearer the tuning pegs.

Let's now discuss scales. All that a scale consists of is a series of notes played in ascending or descending order (going down). The major scale, which has a cheery, bright tone, is the most often used scale in Western music. A fun fact about "The Sound of Music" is that the song "Do-Re-Mi" really sings the notes of a major scale!

What makes scales significant? They resemble the framework of music, actually. Notes from scales are used to build most melodies and harmonies. Knowing scales can make it easier for you to determine what notes work well together and why particular note combinations in music evoke particular feelings.

Understanding your scales is a great way to improve your improvisation as a dulcimer player. As soon as you are aware of the scale that a song is built around, you can play various notes from that scale to either compose original melodies or enhance well-known songs.

Dulcimer Tablature Reading

Let's now discuss something exclusive to our favorite instrument: dulcimer tablature, or simply "tabs". Composing music, especially for fretted instruments, such as the dulcimer, is known as tablature. Especially for novices, it's far simpler to read than traditional sheet music.

What precisely is tablature, then? See your dulcimer strings all flat and pictured on a page. The tablature essentially looks like that.

On your dulcimer, each line represents a string, and the numbers on those lines indicate which fret to play on that particular string.

Here's how to interpret tabs for dulcimers:

1. Your melody string, or the string that is closest to you while playing, is represented by the top line.

2. Your center string is the middle line.

3. Your bass string, which is the one furthest away from you, is the bottom line.

4. The lines' numbers indicate which fret to play. Play on the open string (no fret) when you see a "0".

5. Similar to how words are read on a page, the numerals are read from left to right.

A "3" on the top line, for instance, indicates to "play the 3rd fret on the melody string." Easy enough, huh?

The fact that tablature shows you exactly where to place your fingers is one of its many wonderful features. You don't have to worry about reading rhythms or note names—we'll cover that in a moment. Because of this, it's an excellent tool for novices or for picking up new tunes rapidly.

Time and Rhythm

Okay, so we've spoken about notes, scales, and tablature reading. However, we also need to discuss rhythm, which is another important component of music. The pulse and groove of music are derived from rhythm.

It's what gives you the want to nod or tap your foot in time to a catchy song.

Written music conveys rhythm by using different symbols and note shapes. Here are a few fundamentals:

• A whole note (which appears as an empty oval) has four beats in it.

• A half note has two beats and is an empty oval with a stem.

• A quarter note is a one-beat filled-in oval with a stem.

• An eighth note is a half-beat long filled-in oval with a stem and a flag.

These are the basic rhythms you'll hear most frequently; there are more intricate rhythms as well.

That's one drawback of simple tablature, as you may be thinking, "But wait!

The tablature we just learned about doesn't show rhythm!" While many more complex tabs lack rhythm notation above the tab lines, some do.

To acquire a sense of the rhythm, it is therefore beneficial to listen to recordings of songs as you are learning them.

Developing your time is essential to becoming a proficient dulcimer player. Here are some activities for you to try:

1. Practice using a metronome: Set a metronome to a modest pace, such as 60 beats per minute (you can get free ones online). Make an effort to precisely pluck or strum your dulcimer on every beat. Once you feel more at ease, try strumming two, then four times per beat.

2. Tap along: Try tapping your foot or nodding your head in time with the beat when you're listening to music, any genre of music.

This aids in assimilating the rhythm.

3. Count out loud: To keep yourself on track and aware of where you are in the measure, count the beats aloud while you play: "1, 2, 3, 4, 1, 2, 3, 4."

4. Play along with recordings: Consider picking up some dulcimer music on recordings.

At first, don't stress about hitting every note accurately; instead, concentrate on keeping time with the recording.

Recall that mastering rhythm requires patience and repetition. Don't be scared to start slowly and exercise patience with yourself.

Playing slowly and gradually is preferable to rushing and losing the rhythm.

Bringing Everything Together

This chapter has covered a lot of ground, then! We have studied the fundamentals of rhythm and tempo, learned how to read dulcimer tablature, and discussed musical notes and how they generate scales.

You may be wondering how these parts go together. That's the beauty of music theory, after all: it makes it easier for you to comprehend the fundamental ideas behind the pieces you perform. While honing your dulcimer skills, attempt to pay attention to the following:

• What notes are you using to play? Do you see any patterns or scales?

• How does the piece's rhythm affect how it feels overall?

• Can you begin to identify typical chord shapes or patterns when reading tablature?

If everything seems a little daunting at first, don't worry. What we've discussed here is only the very beginning of the vast topic of music theory.

It's crucial to maintain your curiosity and never stop exploring. You'll notice that these ideas start to come naturally as you explore and learn more.

Recall that mastering music theory is meant to equip you with the knowledge and skills necessary to comprehend, value, and compose music on a deeper level rather than to make learning to play the dulcimer feel like a math lecture.

So enjoy yourself while doing it! Play about, discover new things, and most of all, take pleasure in your dulcimer's lovely melodies.

CHAPTER 5

STARTING WITH A GAME

The fundamentals of holding and strumming your instrument, as well as playing your first notes and chords, are covered in this chapter. If you initially feel a little uncomfortable, don't panic; keep in mind that every great dulcimer player began precisely where you are now. Let's get started and enjoy ourselves!

Grasping and Playing the Dulcimer

Let's start by discussing the proper way to handle a dulcimer. I get what you're thinking: "How hard can it be to hold an instrument?" But you'd be astonished at how much better your playing comfort and sound quality can be when you place your instrument correctly. Let's do this correctly from the beginning!

The Right Position for Playing

1. Either sitting or standing: You can play the dulcimer either way, although, for novices, I

suggest sitting. You have better control and it's more comfortable.

2. Setting Up the Dulcimer: If you are a right-handed person, place the dulcimer on your lap with the tuning pegs facing left. The lower edge of the dulcimer should be pressed on your tummy as it rests comfortably over your thighs.

3. Angle: Slightly slant the dulcimer in your direction. At this angle, you can easily reach all the strings and view the fretboard well.

4. Shoulders Down: Maintain a calm and downcast posture. Happy muscles and nice music are enemies of tension!

5. Back Straight: Sit erect but not rigidly. Maintaining proper posture throughout prolonged playing sessions helps reduce strain and tiredness.

6. Feet Flat: Maintain a flat surface with both feet. You gain balance and stability from this.

Recall that comfort is essential. Whenever something doesn't seem quite right, move to a more comfortable position.

It should feel natural for your dulcimer to be an extension of your body.

Patterns and Techniques for Strumming

Now that you have a flawless grip on your dulcimer, let's discuss strumming. The foundation of dulcimer playing is strum, and knowing a few fundamental methods can help you succeed.

1. Simple Strum: The simplest basic strum is moving your thumb or index finger down and across all of the strings. Sweep down to the lowest string starting from the topmost (closest to you) string. It feels as though you are softly cleaning the strings of dust.

2. Up Strum: After mastering the down strum, attempt an up strum. Beginning with the lowest string, work your way upward. Although a little more difficult, this broadens your playing options.

3. Alternating Strum: Down, up, down, and up are combined at a constant pace. This is the basis for a lot of dulcimer songs.

4. Thumb and Finger Strumming: For down strums, use your thumb, and for up strums, your index finger. This produces a somewhat distinct tone and provides you with more control.

5. Fingerpicking: Although it's not the same as strumming, fingerpicking entails using your thumb and fingers to pluck individual strings. Later chapters will delve deeper into this.

Patterns of Strumming:

Start with these easy designs:

• Four-four times, down, down, down

• Four-four times, Down-Up-Down-Up

• 3/4 time Down-Down-Up

At the start, practice these patterns slowly, paying attention to maintaining a constant rhythm. Try increasing the pace or blending patterns as you get more at ease.

Recall that feeling is just as important to strumming as technique. Try different things until you find what comes naturally to you.

The dulcimer is a versatile instrument that may be played in a variety of ways, which adds to its allure.

Performing Your First Chords and Notes

Okay, you're strumming like a pro and you have perfect posture. Now for the really exciting part: creating songs that people will recognize!

Easy Chords and Melodies

Let's begin with a fairly easy tune that is well-known to all: "Mary Had a Little Lamb." Here is how to play it:

1. Put your index finger on the middle string's first fret.

2. Hit that string; you've hit your first note!

3. Now, without using your fingers, pluck the middle, open string.

4. Again, pluck the open center string.

5. Go back to the middle string's first fret.

6. Three times, pluck the middle string at the first fret.

7. Pluck the middle string twice that is open.

Best wishes! You just performed your first dulcimer melody. Nice, huh?

Let's try a basic chord now. The "open chord" is the simplest chord to play on a dulcimer. Here's how to play it:

1. Strumming all three strings without hitting any frets is all that is required.

2. And that's it! You're striking a note!

In many dulcimer songs, this open chord serves as the "home base" or foundation. It is an excellent place to start learning about how chords function on your particular instrument.

Standard Finger Positioning

You'll pick up increasingly intricate finger movements for various notes and chords as you advance. Here are some pointers to get you going:

1. Press the strings against the frets with the pads of your fingers, not the tips.

2. Don't press too hard or you'll strain your hand; just enough pressure to make a clear sound.

3. Make an effort to keep your fingers curled, with each tip pointing away from the fretboard.

4. Keep your finger close to the fretboard so it's always ready to go when you need it.

5. Practice smoothly and swiftly switching between various finger positions.

Always keep in mind that practicing proper finger placement takes time. If it seems strange at first, don't give up; with practice, your fingers will become more flexible and strong.

A Few Other Pointers for Novices:

1. Start slowly: Although it may be tempting to attempt playing quickly at first, practicing slowly and deliberately can help you form positive habits and muscle memory.

2. Listen intently and take note of the sound you're making. Do your notes sound clear and distinct? If not, change the way you strumming or applying pressure to your fingers.

3. Keep your dulcimer in tune by using a tuner. It can be annoying to play an instrument that is out of tune and difficult to judge whether you are playing correctly.

4. Practice frequently: Ten to fifteen minutes each day is preferable to a single, extended practice once a week.

5. It takes time to learn any instrument, so be patient with yourself. Enjoy the trip and recognize your little wins!

6. Play music you enjoy: While it's crucial to practice scales and exercises, don't forget to play music you adore. It will serve as a motivator and a reminder of your initial motivation for playing.

CHAPTER 6

Learning actual tunes is one of the most fun phases of learning the guitar. This chapter focuses on getting you started with some easy songs that will quickly make you feel like a professional musician. We'll go over folk ballads, hit songs, and even assist you in creating a repertoire of original compositions. Now take out your guitar and let's get started!

Traditional Music and Lyrics

When you're studying the guitar, folk tunes are a great place to start. They frequently have appealing melodies, straightforward chord progressions, and intriguingly narrative lyrics. They're also ideal for novices because they're usually rather understanding if you make a few mistakes!

Simple folk tunes to get you going

Let's begin with some traditional folk tunes that are ideal for novices:

1. Woody Guthrie's "This Land Is Your Land" is an American classic that just requires three chords G, C, and D. This song is excellent for honing your chord changes and strumming techniques.

2. "Blowin' in the Wind" by Bob Dylan: This song, which has three chords (G, C, and D), is a great way to practice fingerpicking or basic strumming patterns.

3. "House of the Rising Sun" by The Animals is a fantastic tune to practice the arpeggio technique and develop finger strength, even though it uses a few extra chords (Am, C, D, F, and E).

4. John Denver's "Leaving on a Jet Plane" is a lovely song with G, C, and D chords that is ideal for honing your rhythm and belting out along as you play.

Easy steps for well-known songs

Now let's use a step-by-step method to dissect the process of learning a song. We'll use Oasis'

pg. 53

"Wonderwall" as an example as it's a well-known song that many people are just learning:

First, learn the chords for "Wonderwall," which are Em7, G, D, and A7sus4. Work on each chord separately until you can transition between them with ease.

Step 2: Learn the strumming pattern "Wonderwall" has the following basic strumming pattern: Down, Down, Up, Up, Down, Up. Start off doing this gently and work your way up to a faster pace.

Step 3: Combine chords and strumming Now, bring the chords and the strumming pattern together. Start slowly and prioritize accuracy over speed.

The fourth step is to become familiar with the song's structure. Verse: Em7 - G - D - A7sus4 (repeat) Chorus: C - D - A7sus4 (repeat)

Step 5: Add the words Sing along after you're at ease with the chords and strumming. It's normal if it seems difficult at first; synchronizing singing and playing takes practice!

Keep in mind that you can use this method to learn any song you like. Enjoy the ride, take your time, and have patience with yourself!

Putting Together a Song Catalog

You should add more songs to your repertoire as you get better at playing the guitar. Possessing a varied repertory enhances your versatility as a musician and adds excitement and intrigue to your practice sessions.

Adding more songs to your playlist

The following advice can help you expand your song library:

1. Investigate many genres; don't stick to one particular kind of music. Sample some pop, rock, country, blues, and even some classical music. You'll learn new skills and expand your musical horizons with each genre.

2. Select a handful of your favorite musicians and learn some of their songs. Learn songs from your favorite artists. Since you'll be listening to music you already enjoy, this might be inspiring.

3. Challenge yourself: While it's a good idea to start with simple songs, as you get better don't be scared to take on parts that are a little bit harder.

You'll develop as a guitarist as a result.

4. Use internet resources: Songsterr, Ultimate Guitar, and YouTube tutorials are great places to locate new music to learn and receive instruction on how to perform it.

5. Become a member of a guitar community. You can meet new people who play the instrument and receive encouragement while you study. You can do this online or in person.

Some advice for rapidly picking up new tunes

Do you want to expand your song library more quickly? The following advice can help hasten the learning process:

1. Before delving into the minute nuances, familiarize yourself with the song's core chord pattern. This provides you with a strong base on which to grow.

2. To enhance your timing and rhythm, practice using a metronome. Gradually pick up the pace as you get more at ease, starting slowly.

3. Divide the song into manageable chunks rather than attempting to memorize it all at once. Divide it into verse, chorus, and bridge sections, and focus on each piece alone.

4. Pay attention to problem areas: Determine the difficult passages in the song and work on them alone. The remaining parts of the song will come together more readily once you've mastered these challenging passages.

5. Play along with the recording After you've mastered the fundamentals, consider following the original recording. This aids in perfecting the song's tempo and vibe.

6. Take a video of yourself with your phone or another inexpensive recording equipment.

You can find areas that require improvement by using a listener's perspective.

7. Try teaching a song to someone else when you believe you have mastered it. This procedure might assist in confirming your comprehension and pointing out any knowledge gaps.

Recall that developing a repertory requires patience and time. You should not lose hope if you are not able to pick up songs as rapidly as you would like to because everyone learns differently. Embrace the journey and acknowledge your accomplishments, regardless of how minor they may appear.

Your ability to pick up new songs will get better as you keep learning and developing as a guitarist.

It will become easier to learn new material as you become familiar with popular chord progressions, strumming patterns, and song structures.

So, don't give up! You'll soon have a long list of songs under your belt and be prepared to perform for friends, family, and maybe even a live audience. Who knows?

CHAPTER 7

EXAMINING VARIOUS PLAYING METHODS

You've reached one of the most thrilling sections of your guitar career. We're going to delve into the realm of various playing methods that will elevate your guitar abilities beyond proficiency. Now that you have your guitar in hand, settle down, and let's explore some amazing techniques for getting it to sing!

Using your fingers and your flatpack

First, let's review two essential guitar-playing skills that any player should possess: fingerpicking and flatpicking. It's critical to comprehend and practice both of these playing techniques because they can drastically alter the sound of your guitar.

An overview of fingerpicking methods

Using your fingertips, fingernails, or even tiny instruments called fingerpicks, you can directly pluck the strings in fingerpicking, sometimes referred to as fingerstyle.

With the help of this technique, you can play numerous strings at once to produce rich, complex sounds that can transform your guitar into a miniature orchestra.

Try this easy activity to get your fingerpicking skills started:

1. Thumb (p) resting on the sixth string (low E)

2. Put the third string (G) under your index finger (i).

3. Put the second string (B) with your middle finger (m).

4. Lastly, your first string (high E) on your ring finger (a).

Try now to pluck these strings in the following order: p, i, m, a, m, i. Continue in this manner, gradually at first. You can start experimenting with different patterns and using all six strings as you get more at ease.

Recall that fingerpicking takes practice to become proficient, so don't give up if it seems strange at first. Your fingers will acquire muscle memory with practice, so you'll be fingerpicking like a pro in no time!

The fundamentals of flatpicking

Conversely, there is flatpicking. Using a pick, which is another name for a plectrum, you strike the strings with this technique. Playing single-note melodies, rapid runs, and strumming chords with a clear, defined sound are all made possible by flatpicking.

In case you've never used a pick before, here are some pointers to get you going:

1. About halfway down the pick's length, place your thumb and index finger between them.

2. Avoid getting too firm with your grasp; you'll have better control and avoid getting tired.

3. On each string, begin by practicing downstrokes, and then upstrokes. After you're at ease, switch between picking up and down (also known as alternating picking).

Try this exercise: Play a scale by choosing notes alternately, being sure to make each note even and distinct. As you get more comfortable, start out slowly and progressively pick up the pace.

For instance, bluegrass, rock, and country music all heavily rely on flatpicking. It makes speed and accuracy possible it may be more difficult to do with fingerpicking alone.

Including Embellishments

After going over the fundamentals, let's add some decoration to the piece. These are minor details that can give your playing more personality and emotion.

Drawbacks and slants

With the help of hammer-ons and pull-offs, you may produce a fluid, legato sound by playing notes without picking each one.

For a head-on:

1. Play a standard note.

2. Use a finger on your fretting hand to "hammer" down on a higher fret on the same string while it's still ringing.

Regarding a pull-off:

1. Press a fretted note.

2. To produce a lower note on the same string while it is still ringing, "pull" your fretting finger off the string and pluck it gently.

Try this: Hammer onto the seventh fret after playing the fifth fret on the B string. Play the seventh fret and pull off to the fifth, then flip it around. Work on this until it sounds fluid and both notes are at the same volume.

twists and slides

You can express yourself more and find your inner blues or rock musician by using bends and slides.

Regarding a slide:

1. Play a note.

2. Slide your finger up or down to another fret without raising it.

To bend:

1. Play a note.

2. Raise the pitch by pushing the string sideways.

3. You have the option of doing quarter, half, or full bends, which raise the pitch by one semitone, one whole tone, or more.

Play the G string at the 7th fret, then slide up to the 9th fret for a fun workout. Play the ninth fret once again and execute a complete bend. For a cool effect, slowly release the bent!

Complex Strumming Techniques

Okay, so let's talk about how to improve your rhythm skills with some more complex strumming methods.

sophisticated strumming methods

Simple down-up strumming is wonderful, but you'll want to add more intricate patterns to make your rhythm playing come to life. Here are some to give a go:

1. Folk and country songs are popular with the "Boom-Chick" sound. Using your thumb, pluck the chord's bass note (boom), and then strum the higher strings (chick).

2. The "Skipstrum": Try "skipping" some of the downstrum or upstrum rather than hitting every string. This produces an intriguing, more syncopated rhythm.

3. Palm Muting: When strumming, lightly place the side of your picking hand on the strings close to the bridge. This produces a percussion sound that is muted and perfect for rock and metal.

Including changes in rhythm

After mastering these methods, it's time to experiment with the beat itself. Here are a few ideas for introducing variation:

1. Accents: Play some strums louder to emphasize them. This has the power to entirely alter a rhythm's vibe.

2. Ghost Strums: They create texture without contributing loud notes. They can be extremely faint strums or even just muted scratches.

3. Percussive hits: To create sounds akin to drums, strike the guitar's body or strings with your plucking hand.

Try this pattern: Down, Down-Up, Up-Down-Up. On the first down, play a palm mute; on the second down, play an accent; and on the final up, play a ghost strum. Start out slowly and pick up the pace as you become more comfortable.

Recall that persistent, patient practice is essential to becoming proficient in these methods. Instead of attempting to learn everything at once, concentrate on one technique at a time and make sure you understand it thoroughly before moving on.

Additionally, don't be scared to try new things and blend various methods. Consider attempting a flatpicked melody with some bends and slides, or a fingerpicked rhythm with some hammer-ons. There are countless options!

Finally, have a listen to a diverse range of guitarists and attempt to identify the methods they employ. Is there any fingerpicking in a traditional song? The intricate strumming patterns found in a song of reggae? The turns and slides of a solo in the blues? Just as vital as training your fingers is training your ears.

Alright, people, this chapter has covered a lot of ground! You have a toolbox full of new abilities to practice and apply to your playing now that you know everything from the fundamentals of fingerpicking and flatpicking to some very sophisticated techniques.

Recall that mastering these methods requires time, so be kind to yourself. Appreciate the little things, like the first time you master a challenging strumming pattern or the seamless switch between fingerpicking and flatpicking. Every piece of development is a step in the direction of your goal of becoming a guitarist.

CHAPTER 8
UNDERSTANDING CHORDS AND SCALES

Greetings and welcome to Chapter 8, where we will be exploring the mysteries of scales and chords.

If some of these ideas seem a little overwhelming, don't worry; we'll simplify them into manageable chunks. You'll be running scales and strumming chords like an expert by the conclusion of this chapter!

Let's begin with the fundamentals: what are scales and chords specifically? Consider these to be the fundamental elements of music. Scales are notes performed one after the other, whereas chords are groupings of notes played simultaneously. Both are necessary to play dulcimer melodies and harmonies.

Basic Dulcimer Chords

Okay, let's start by talking about chords. Because of the dulcimer's special fret arrangement and tuning, performing chords on it differs slightly from playing other stringed instruments. But don't be alarmed by it; in fact, it makes playing some chords simpler!

The major, minor, and seventh chords are the most often encountered chords. Let's dissect them:

1. Major Chords: Major chords sound upbeat and cheery. They are frequently the easiest to perform on the dulcimer. For instance, you only need to strum all of the open strings to play a D major chord. Simple as pie, huh?

2. Minor Chords: The sound of a minor chord is more eerie or enigmatic. On the dulcimer, they're a little more difficult, but still doable. For

example, to play an A minor chord, strum all the strings and fret the first string at the third fret.

3.7th chords: Frequently employed in jazz and blues, 7th chords provide a little bit of tension. They can be a little more intricate when played on the dulcimer, but they still have a beautiful flavor. For example, fretting the first string at the first fret and the third string at the second fret will allow you to play a G7 chord.

Let's now discuss chord progression and playing techniques. Practice, practice, and more practice are the keys here! Begin by becoming accustomed to each chord on its own. Make sure every note is audible when you strum slowly.

After you're comfortable with it, try alternating between two chords. For instance, change the key to G major (fret the first string at the seventh fret) from D major (all open strings).

It's very natural for your transitions to seem a little sluggish and slow at first! If you persist, your fingers will eventually begin to recall where they belong. Using a slow metronome and switching chords every four beats is a useful workout.

You can pick up the tempo or switch chords more frequently as you become more at ease.

Recall that expertly executed chord transitions are the key to performing songs with a polished, stage-worthy sound.

Therefore, if it takes some time to master, don't give up; your perseverance will be rewarded!

Examining Scales

Now that we understand chords, let's explore the realm of scales. The building blocks of melody and scales can greatly aid in your comprehension of the compositional process. Furthermore, learning scales is an excellent method to increase your fretboard familiarity and finger dexterity.

First, let's discuss the two most popular kinds of scales:

1. Major Scales: The basis of Western music is the major scale. It sounds cheery and cheerful, like

"Do-Re-Mi" from The Sound of Music. Playing a major scale on the dulcimer is not too difficult. A D major scale, for instance, would be played by starting on the open first string (D) and moving up the fretboard one fret at a time until you reached the subsequent D note.

2. Minor Scales: Minor scales sound more ominous or enigmatic.

They are made by decreasing the major scale's third, sixth, and seventh notes by a half step, or one fret on a dulcimer. For example, the fifth fret of the first string would be the beginning of an A minor scale.

But there's still more! Let's investigate a few more fascinating scales:

3. Pentatonic Scales: Known for their five notes, pentatonic scales are incredibly common in rock, blues, and folk music. They're easy to learn and sound fantastic, which makes them ideal for improvisation. The pentatonic scales are major

and minor. On a dulcimer, for instance, a G major pentatonic scale would be G, A, B, D, and E.

4. Modal Scales: Each mode has its own distinct flavor due to the fact that modal scales are developed from major scales but begin on different notes. The most popular modes are Dorian, Phrygian, Lydian, Mixolydian, Aeolian (which is the same as the natural minor scale), Locrian, and Ionian, which is the same as the major scale. Every option has a unique tone and can give your playing some intriguing new hues.

"This is all great, but how do I actually use these scales?" is a valid question, I know. Here are several examples:

1. Improvisation: You can use notes from a scale to compose your own tunes if you are familiar with it. Try creating a melody using notes from the relevant scale and following a straightforward chord sequence.

2. Recognizing songs: Notes from a specific scale are often used to construct tunes. Understanding

your scales will make it easier for you to identify tunes by ear.

3. Writing original music: Scales provide you with a structure to operate inside when you're writing. They resemble a set of notes that you can be sure will work well together.

4. Playing lead: Being aware of your scales can help you confidently travel the fretboard when you wish to take a solo during a jam session with friends.

Recall that mastering the scales does not entail aimlessly moving up and down the fretboard.

It's about internalizing the feel and sound of many musical "flavors." As you practice, make an effort to truly hear the distinctive qualities of each scale.

Try this entertaining exercise: Take a scale (D major, for example) and play it gently up and down your dulcimer. Try again with the same notes, but a new arrangement. Perhaps play two notes down and three notes up, or hop around a bit.

Even though you're still working with the D major scale, you're now composing your own songs!

You'll begin to see how chords and scales are related when you experiment with them. Scales contain notes that can be utilized to build melodies that fit over chords, which are constructed from those notes. It resembles a stunning musical ecosystem!

It's not necessary for you to grasp everything at once. Understanding chords and scales is a process rather than a final goal.

Start with the fundamentals: the major scale, and a few major and minor chords. Add more to your repertoire gradually as you become more at ease with those.

Never forget that enjoying yourself is the most crucial factor. Consider adding additional scale lines or chords to tunes you are already familiar with. Play around with various combos.

The dulcimer is an incredibly expressive instrument, and learning chords and scales will allow you to explore a whole new range of melodic options.

CHAPTER 9

In learning to play this lovely instrument, we've gone a long way, don't we? I know you're feeling pretty good about yourself by now, but when you start playing with other people, that's when the real magic begins. We'll delve into some advice for performing with other musicians, discuss the pleasures of jamming with friends, and even address ways to become more active in the dulcimer community in this chapter. Now take out your dulcimer and let's get started!

Playing Music with Pals

Making music with other people is a really unique experience. It's similar to conversing, but melodies and rhythms are used in place of words. Not only are you making music when you jam with pals, but you're also forming a bond that may be immensely satisfying and enjoyable!

"But I'm not good enough to play with others yet!" is probably what some of you are thinking, and let me cut you off there.

The delight of jamming lies in the fact that it's not about perfection but rather about having fun and picking each other's brains. Actually, one of the finest ways to get better at something is to play with other people.

How then do you begin? It's easy: arrange a cozy area, contact a few buddies who enjoy music, and just start performing! First, don't stress too much about the structure. Start with some well-known, basic songs and follow your musical inspiration. Recall that the purpose of music is to foster connection and enjoyment.

Advice on Performing with Other Artists

Now that you're eager to start jamming, let's discuss some pointers to enhance your group playing experience:

1. Play less and listen more: This may seem obvious, but it's important. Playing with other people involves more than just you.

Observe others and attempt to harmonize your tone with theirs.

2. Keep time: The foundation of any successful jam session is a constant rhythm. It's acceptable to take a backseat and concentrate on maintaining a steady beat rather than attempting to play intricate tunes if you're not secure in your time.

3. Jamming isn't a competition, so take turns. Give each person their moment to shine. Take turns taking the initiative and supporting one another.

4. Acquire a repertoire of well-known songs that many musicians are familiar with. This will serve as a basis for your jam sessions and a terrific icebreaker.

5. Be receptive to many styles: Getting to hear new music is one of the pleasures of performing

with others. If you accept the variety, you can find a new genre that you love!

6. Remind yourself that everyone makes errors occasionally, so don't be scared to make them.

If you make a mistake, simply continue. Often, others may not even notice a mistake that would seem to be obvious.

Recognizing Group Musical Dynamics

You have total control over the music's overall feel, volume, and tempo when you perform solo. However, these components become a team endeavor in a group context. This is the point at which knowledge of musical dynamics becomes essential.

In music, dynamics are variations in sound intensity, such as loudness or softness. This idea also applies to how each player or instrument enhances the overall sound in a group situation. Here are some important things to remember:

1. Check your volume balance to make sure you're not overpowering other people or speaking too softly.

It all comes down to identifying the ideal location where each person's contribution is obvious.

2. Lead vs. rhythm section: You'll find that players often find themselves in rhythm and lead parts by instinct. It's your responsibility as a rhythm player to set a solid foundation so that the lead may shine. Be careful not to overrun the rhythm section when playing lead.

3. Declining and rising tones are known as crescendos and diminuendos, and they may give your music a lot of expressive depth. As a group, try incorporating these for some incredibly dynamic playing.

4. In this entertaining approach known as "call and response," one player or group "calls" with a melodic phrase, and another "responds" with a phrase that complements the first. It's a fantastic method to infuse conversation into your songs.

5. Tempo adjustments: Changing the tempo might make your music more engaging, but make sure everyone is on the same page.

Having a chosen leader who can announce these changes can be beneficial.

Recall that the objective is to produce a unified sound where each player's contribution enriches the composition as a whole. You'll be astounded by the rich, full sound you can produce together once you get the hang of it, even though it might take some practice.

Taking Part in Festivals and Dulcimer Circles

Why not step up your jamming with pals now that you feel at ease doing so? Participating in dulcimer festivals and circles is a great way to meet people in the larger dulcimer community, pick up new skills, and become fully immersed in the vibrant culture that surrounds this instrument.

Regular gatherings of dulcimer players, known as "dulcimer circles," take place at community centers, music stores, or even private homes. Players of various skill levels are typically warmly welcomed into these circles.

They're excellent locations for group practice, song learning, and learning advice from more seasoned musicians.

On the other hand, festivals are bigger occasions that frequently take place over multiple days. Workshops, performances, jam sessions, and vendor areas where you can view (and possibly purchase) new instruments and accessories are usually featured. A dulcimer player's fantasy is festivals; just picture yourself surrounded by hundreds of fellow aficionados who are all there to honor this amazing instrument!

Locating Local Groups of Dulcimers

How do you discover these get-togethers with dulcimers, then? Here are some pointers:

1. Look online: Local music groups are frequently listed on websites such as meetup.com.

Additionally, search for local Facebook groups or forums dedicated to dulcimers.

2. Ask at your neighborhood record store; they may even arrange get-togethers and are frequently knowledgeable about the local music scenes.

3. Seek out folk music societies: There is often a crossover between the folk music communities of Dulcimer players. These associations may have leads on groups dedicated to dulcimers.

4. Go to a festival: Folk music festivals typically provide information on local groups, even if they're not exclusively for dulcimers.

5. Create your own: Why not create a group if you are unable to locate one? Send out feelers to see who's interested in your community.

Getting Ready for and Enjoying Holidays

I strongly advise you to go to a dulcimer festival, and if you do, here are some pointers to help you get the most out of it:

1. Make a plan in advance by selecting the workshops and concerts you wish to attend after reviewing the festival schedule. Popular classes tend to fill up fast!

2. Bring your instrument: Having your dulcimer with you allows you to participate if you feel comfortable, even if you aren't comfortable playing with others just yet.

3. Make sensible packing choices: Having a water bottle, some snacks, and comfy shoes will help you stay energized all day.

4. Keep an open mind: Festivals are excellent venues for picking up new skills or fashions.

Try workshops that are a little bit outside of your comfort zone without fear.

5. Participate in the jams: A lot of events feature spaces set aside for unofficial jam sessions. These are excellent locations to practice playing in a relaxed setting with other people.

6. Speak with people: Most people who play the Dulcimer are amiable. Don't be afraid to start a

chat; you might meet some new people and get yourself a playmate!

7. Take things slow; there is a lot to see and do at festivals, which can be daunting.

It's acceptable to take pauses or even miss a few sessions if you're experiencing fatigue.

Recall that having fun is the most crucial factor. Playing with others is all about sharing the joy of music, whether you're at a large festival, dulcimer circle, or just jamming with pals. Thus, go forth, establish a connection with other dulcimer fans, and collaborate to create some lovely music!

CHAPTER 10

Greetings and welcome to Chapter 10, where we will discuss the important subject of taking good care of your beloved dulcimer. Whether you're a novice or an experienced player, maintaining your instrument properly will keep it in excellent condition for many years to come. Now let's get started and learn how to maintain the greatest possible appearance and soun

d for your dulcimer!

Upkeep and Cleaning

Let's face it — your dulcimer is going to gather dust, fingerprints, and maybe even a few coffee stains over time. But don't worry! With a little TLC, you can keep it looking as good as new.

Routine cleaning practices:

1. Dust regularly: Think of your dulcimer as a fragile piece of furniture. Use a soft, lint-free cloth

to carefully wipe clean the entire instrument after each playing session.

This prevents dust from collecting up and potentially hurting the sound.

2. Clean the strings: Your strings are the heart of your dulcimer's sound, so keep them clean! After playing, rub a clean towel along the length of each string to remove oils and debris from your fingertips.

3. Use caution when polishing: Use a wood polish made specifically for musical instruments for a deeper clean. Use a gentle cloth to apply it sparingly, being sure to always go with the wood's grain. Recall that when it comes to polish, less is more!

4. Remember the fretboard: If your dulcimer has one, pay close attention to it as well. Wipe between the frets with a little damp cloth and quickly dry with another clean, dry cloth.

5. Keep it dry: Your dulcimer is not a friend of humidity. Keep your instrument out of the direct sun and heat sources at all times.

Tips for long-term care:

1. Invest in a good case: When your dulcimer isn't being played, a good case is its best friend.

It guards against temperature changes, dust, and unintentional bumps.

2. Watch the temperature: Wooden instruments can suffer greatly from extremely high or low temperatures. Keep your dulcimer away from radiators and hot cars.

3. Excessive dryness in the air may necessitate the use of a humidifier in the case of your instrument. Just watch out not to go overboard—too much or too little moisture can have equally negative effects.

4. Frequent inspections: Examine your dulcimer closely every several months. Look for any cracks, loose pieces, or other wear-and-tear indicators.

5. Replacing strings: Avoid waiting for them to break! To keep the best possible sound quality, replace them on a regular basis. How frequently? For frequent players, a decent rule of thumb is every three to six months, depending on how frequently you play.

Troubleshooting Typical Problems

There may be a few bumps in the road, even with the finest care. Let's examine a few typical issues and potential solutions.

Recognizing and addressing typical issues:

1. When your strings buzz, it's usually an indication that they're too close to the frets.

Consider lowering the bridge a little bit. You may need to get the neck alignment checked if that is ineffective.

2. Tuning issues: Make sure your dulcimer's tuning pegs are tight before attempting to keep it out of tune. A dab of wood glue in the peg hole will help if they're loose.

Additionally, confirm that the strings you're playing on your instrument have the proper gauge.

3. Wood cracks: Wood glue and a little touch can occasionally be used to seal small fractures in the wood. Larger cracks, on the other hand, or those close to important places like the soundboard, might need to be professionally repaired.

4. Sounds that rattle: When you play and hear an enigmatic rattling, look for any loose bits. Find any screws and tighten them, but be careful—overtightening might lead to damage.

5. Wear on frets: Frets can deteriorate with time, particularly in sections that are played often.

It may be time for a fret job if you observe uneven frets or trouble playing in specific positions.

6. Warped wood: Prolonged exposure to high humidity or temperatures typically causes significant warping.

If you address the environmental conditions, minor warping may self-correct; but, severe cases will require professional assistance.

When to get expert assistance:

Although it's wonderful to be able to solve small problems on your own, there are instances when it's advisable to hire professionals. In the following circumstances, seeking expert assistance is advised:

1. Structural damage: An expert should inspect any fractures or separations in the instrument's body.

2. Neck alignment problems: A skilled luthier should handle this if the neck appears twisted or misaligned.

3. Replacement frets are a delicate task best left to experts, while you can perform some fret maintenance yourself.

4. Bridge issues: Have your bridge inspected if it appears to be lifting or is out of alignment. A

badly adjusted bridge can lead to a variety of tuning and playability problems.

5. Refinishing: Want to change the appearance of your dulcimer? Refinishing is an intricate procedure that is best left to the expertise of a professional.

6. When in doubt: Rather than taking a chance on breaking your instrument, it's always best to see a professional for any repair or maintenance task if you're hesitant about it.

Recall that a local luthier or music store might be a very helpful resource. If you have any concerns, don't be afraid to seek help or bring your dulcimer in for a check-up.

Maintaining your dulcimer is a kind gesture. It's about keeping the lovely instrument that makes you so happy and it's capacity to produce great music. Your dulcimer can accompany you on your musical journey for a lifetime if you give it regular care and attention.

CHAPTER 11

You've reached one of the most important stages in your development as a proficient guitarist.

Thus far, we've covered a lot of ground, from picking out your first guitar to mastering fundamental chords and playing methods.

It's time to discuss practice and growth, two things that have the power to make or destroy your success.

It's a fact that no one becomes an instant guitar legend. Even legendary musicians like Eddie Van Halen, Eric Clapton, and Jimi Hendrix devoted endless hours to perfecting their craft. However, don't be intimidated by it!

Practice may be highly productive, pleasurable, and gratifying when done correctly.

Now let's get started on how to maximize your practice time and monitor your development as you go.

Establishing a Practice Schedule

You must first establish a practice schedule.

I understand that you may be thinking, "Ugh, routine sounds boring!" but I promise that practicing in an organized manner can actually make it more enjoyable and eff

ective. This is the reason why:

1. It keeps you focused: You're less inclined to squander time aimlessly when you have a plan in place.

2. It guarantees balanced development: A solid practice program addresses every facet of your playing, from theory to technique.

3. It cultivates discipline: Developing a routine aids in the development of consistency, which is essential for mastering any skill.

So, how can one design a practice regimen that works? Let's dissect it:

Establishing Practice Objectives

Knowing what you want to achieve is essential before you start practicing. Establishing attainable objectives helps provide focus and direction to your practice sessions. The following advice can help you create practice goals that work:

1. Be precise. Rather than aiming to "get better at guitar," for example, try something more like "learn to play the intro to 'Sweet Child O' Mine' smoothly."

2. Make them quantifiable: How will you determine whether a goal has been met? For instance, "Be able to play the C, G, and D chords without looking at my fingers."

3. Establish both short- and long-term objectives; a balance will help you stay motivated. Learning a new chord this week could be a short-term objective; performing at an open mic night in six months could be a long-term one.

4. Put your goals down in writing; there's a certain strength in doing so.

It helps you maintain accountability and gives them a more genuine sense.

Keep in mind that while your goals should push you, they shouldn't be unbearably hard. Finding the ideal balance between pushing oneself and having fun with the process is crucial.

Finding a Balance Between Play and Practice

Here's a secret that many inexperienced guitarists fail to realize: playing and practicing are two very different things, and you need both to develop as a musician.

Practice is a concentrated, organized effort on particular abilities or parts. Here is where you hone your skills, address your areas of weakness, and challenge yourself to get better. Conversely, while playing, you can let go, sing along to your favorite tunes, or just have fun.

Finding the ideal balance between the two is essential to maintaining motivation and moving forward steadily. Here's how to easily achieve that balance:

1. Warm up, then focus on your present objectives and difficulties to begin your practice session in an organized manner.

2. Playtime at the end of the session: Take this opportunity to play around or apply what you've learned.

You can have the best of both worlds with this method. Not only are you improving your abilities, but you're also remembering why you initially picked up the guitar: it's just fun!

Monitoring Your Development

Okay, so you've established your objectives and are practicing on a regular basis. However, how can you tell whether you're genuinely getting better? This is where keeping track of your development is useful.

Not only is it empowering to realize how far you've gone, but it's also important to pinpoint areas that still require improvement and modify your practice regimen accordingly.

Maintaining a Practice Notebook

Maintaining a practice notebook is one of the finest strategies to monitor your development. You don't have to treat this like a diary unless that's how you want it to be. You have complete control over how extensive or basic your practice journal is.

The following are some items you may wish to include:

1. When and for how long you practiced

2. What you practiced (such as tunes, chords, and scales)

3. Any innovations or "aha!" experiences

4. obstacles you encountered

5. Objectives for the upcoming meeting

You can utilize a notepad, an app on your phone for taking notes, or even a practice-tracking program. Maintaining consistency with it is crucial.

Here's a little secret: go back through your notebook on days when you don't feel like you're progressing.

Even though it doesn't always feel like it at the time, you'll be shocked at how far you've come.

Assessing Your Advancement

Even while your practice notebook provides you with a daily overview of your development, it's crucial to take a step back and assess your overall advancement on a regular basis. To that end, here are a few methods:

1. Record yourself: Play the same piece or workout on video every month or so. You'll get more and more proficient in terms of timing, tone, and general musicality over time.

2. Go back to earlier material: Try performing songs or workouts that used to be difficult for you. You may be shocked at how much simpler they've gotten.

3. Obtain feedback: If you're enrolled in classes, your instructor might offer insightful commentary on your development. If you're self-taught, you might want to look into attending a local meetup group or joining an online guitar community where you can show off your skills and receive helpful criticism.

4. Try it on yourself: Make little tasks based on your objectives. See if you can play all five chords in a row without any hesitation, for instance, if your aim is to learn them.

Recall that progress isn't always straight-line. You may feel like you're making tremendous progress some weeks and stalling others. That is quite typical! The secret is to persevere with consistency.

A Few Concluding Thoughts to Encourage

Before we close this chapter, I would want to share a few ideas with you:

1. It's a journey, not a sprint, to learn the guitar, so have patience with yourself. Take pleasure in the procedure!

2. Honor little accomplishments: Did you successfully execute that challenging chord change? That is certainly cause for celebration!

3. Avoid comparing your guitar journey to that of others; it is exclusively yours. Pay attention to your own development rather than how you compare to others.

4. Change things up: Don't be scared to make changes to your routine if you're getting bored with it. Consider taking on a fun challenge for yourself, trying out a new practice approach, or learning a new genre.

5. Remind yourself why you picked up the guitar in the first place on days when practicing seems like a chore. To get inspired, consider turning on some of your favorite guitar music.

CHAPTER 12

You've worked really hard, developed your abilities, and produced some incredible music.

It's finally here: the thrilling (and occasionally nerve-wracking) part: releasing your song to the public! We'll cover how to get ready for shows, deal with those annoying butterflies in the stomach, and even take a peek at recording in this chapter. Now grab your instrument, inhale deeply, and let's get started!

Getting Ready for a Performance

Okay, so congratulations on your upcoming gig! Be it a full-fledged performance or an open mic night at your neighborhood coffee shop, preparation is essential. The following advice can help you prepare:

1. I know, I know, you've heard this a million times: practice, practice, practice.

On the other hand, you'll feel more assured on stage if you are at ease with your topic.

Go over your list of songs over and again until you can listen to it while you sleep (though maybe don't do that, as your roommates might not like it).

2. Create a set list by selecting tracks that highlight your best qualities and work well together.

Think about the tone you want to set and the intensity you want to keep up during your performance.

3. Verify that all of your equipment is in working order. Replace those worn-out strings, tune-up, and remember to bring extra drumsticks or picks if necessary. Make sure any electronic equipment is functioning properly before using it, and carry extra batteries and cables.

4. Set yourself up for success by taking some time to picture yourself performing with assurance and the crowd applauding. Although it may seem a little woo-woo, positive thinking may significantly increase your self-assurance.

5. Get enough rest the night before your performance to ensure a decent night's sleep. When you go on stage, you want to be energized and invigorated!

Getting Rid of Performance Anxiety

Alright, let us address the most pressing issue - stage fright. You're not alone if you're feeling uneasy—even seasoned performers experience anxiety occasionally! The following techniques will assist you in controlling your nerves:

1. Breathe deeply: You tend to breathe quickly and shallowly when you're anxious. Before you step onto the stage, take a few long, deliberate breaths. It will help your brain receive more oxygen and help you relax.

2. Reframe your anxiety by telling yourself, "I'm excited!" Rather than, "I'm so nervous!" Since excitement and anxiety share many physiological similarities, this mental change can help you use your anxiety constructively.

3. Keep your eyes on your music and not the listeners; after all, you are there to share your creativity. Put more of your attention on the feelings and narrative in your music rather than on what other people may be thinking.

4. Perform as often as you can. The more you perform, the more at ease you'll feel. Play for your loved ones at first, then work your way up to bigger crowds.

5. Talk to yourself positively by treating yourself as you would a close friend. Confidence-boosting statements like "You're going to rock this!" and "You've got this!" can really help.

Some Advice for a Great Performance

Now that you're feeling less anxious and a little more prepared, let's talk about how to really nail your performance:

1. Establish a connection with your audience by smiling, making eye contact, and interacting with them in between songs. You and the audience will both feel more at ease if you joke about a little.

2. Be true to yourself: On stage, don't try to be someone you're not. Your individuality is what makes you distinctive, so be true to who you are.

3. Resolve errors amicably: Don't lose your cool if you strike the wrong note or miss a line.

The audience won't even notice most of the time. Just forward with confidence.

4. Make use of the stage: Make use of any available space for movement! You may convey more emotion in your music and maintain audience interest by incorporating small movements.

5. Express gratitude to the audience for their support. Saying "thank you" is a great technique to establish a good rapport with your audience.

Putting Your Music on Tape

Okay, so let's talk about preserving your musical magic for future generations to enjoy (and possibly your future devoted admirers). Although recording your music can sound intimidating, it's now easier than ever thanks to modern technology.

Here are some fundamental recording methods to get you going:

1. Select the recording technique you want to use. Here are your options. For short demos, you may set up a home studio with a computer, audio interface, and microphone. Alternatively, you could get a portable digital recorder for higher-quality recordings.

2. Locate a quiet area because recordings with background noise are not excellent. Locate the quietest space in your home. Surprisingly,

clothes-filled closets can be an excellent way to reduce echo!

3. Discover your equipment: Invest some time in learning the fundamentals of your recording setup, regardless matter whether you're using a phone app or a full-fledged DAW (Digital Audio Workstation).

4. If you're new to recording, start out simply by using only your voice and one instrument.

You can experiment with layering different songs as you get more at ease.

5. Keep an eye on the levels. If your recording is too loud, it will sound distorted, and if it is too quiet, a lot of background noise will come through. Your loudest portions should peak at roughly -6 dB.

6. Make several attempts; don't aim for perfection the first time. Perform each song multiple times, then select your best take (or blend the greatest elements from various takes).

7. Learn the fundamentals of editing: Even small changes, like cutting the beginning and ending of your track or altering the level, can have a significant impact on the finished output.

Playing Music for Others

Now that you've done some recording and live performances, it's time to promote your music! Here are a few methods for getting the world to hear your music:

1. Social media: You may share quick videos or live performances on sites like Facebook, Instagram, and TikTok.

Utilize pertinent hashtags to make your music more discoverable.

2. Music streaming platforms: Independent musicians can post their songs to Sound Cloud, Apple Music, Spotify, and other services. Investigate distribution options that allow your music to appear on several platforms.

3. YouTube: Make a channel and post your live performances or music videos there. In order to

interact with viewers, you may also use YouTube to post instructional or behind-the-scenes videos.

4. Local music scene: Participate in the scene in your area. Go to open mics, connect with other artists on social media, and join neighborhood music groups.

5. Make a website: Having a website allows fans to easily access your songs, tour schedule, and merchandise.

6. Cooperate: You can reach new listeners and produce interesting new music by teaming up with other musicians.

7. Be dependable: Providing continuous information keeps readers interested. Try posting content on a regular basis, even if it's only a quick update or video.

CONLUSION

With its lengthy history and deep cultural significance, the Appalachian dulcimer provides a distinctive and approachable entry point into the world of music for those just starting out. It is a great option for many different musical genres because of its straightforward but adaptable design. Picking the appropriate instrument and necessary extras like picks and cases is made easier by having a basic understanding of the dulcimer's anatomy, which includes its fretboard and various shapes.

Dulcimer tuning is simple, with basic tunings like D-A-D and D-A-A being essential.

Tuning the instrument on a regular basis guarantees optimal sound quality. Understanding the fundamentals of rhythm, notes, and scales sets the stage for mastering dulcimer tablature and time.

Learning the right stance, basic chords and melodies, and strumming methods are all part of learning to play. Folk tunes and easy songs make appropriate beginning selections, and developing a repertoire facilitates the speedy acquisition of new songs. Playing takes on more depth as one experiment with methods like fingerpicking, flatpicking, and ornamentation like hammer-ons and slides.

Gaining an understanding of major, minor, and pentatonic scales as well as chords enhances the musical experience. Playing with others promotes community and musical development, whether in smaller groups or at festivals and dulcimer circles. The longevity of the dulcimer can be ensured by regular cleaning and taking care of common problems.

Continuous improvement is facilitated by developing a practice regimen with predetermined objectives and documenting advancement in a journal. The journey of studying the Appalachian dulcimer culminates in performing and sharing music—from conquering nervousness to recording and sharing with others.

This book inspires a lifetime love of music and offers a thorough tutorial for learning the instrument, covering everything from the fundamentals to sophisticated methods.

Made in the USA
Middletown, DE
10 September 2024

60630502R00066